BEYOND WORDS

30 Day Devotion with Piano Worship

YOUNGMIN YOU

All Scripture quotations, unless otherwise indicated, are taken from the Holy Bible, New International Version®, NIV®. Copyright ©1973, 1978, 1984, 2011 by Biblica, Inc.™ Used by permission of Zondervan.
All rights reserved worldwide. www.zondervan.com
The "NIV" and "New International Version" are trademarks registered in the United States Patent and Trademark Office by Biblica, Inc.™

Cover Design by Yuliya Mokhan
Interior Design by Dennis Miru

TO

_____

FROM

_____

DATE

_____

DEDICATION

To my Parents, who taught me to
"rejoice always, pray continually, and
give thanks in all circumstances".

FORWARD

In the Summer of 2018, God prompted me to start a 365 Day, 1 Minute Worship on my Instagram.

My heart was in it, but unfortunately, my hands were not. At that point in time, I was averaging 7 hours a day on the piano, and started to experience some serious hand issues. Issues that would force me to quit after Day 182.

But in those 182 days of worshipping with people all around the world for just 1 minute each morning, I saw how desperately we all need reminding of God's great love for us, some encouragement, and some time to slow down and really connect with our Heavenly Father.

I may have "failed" at my 365 day challenge, but the idea of 1 Minute Worship has stayed in my heart, and served as my inspiration for this 30-Day Devotional.

Just like other devotions, each day includes scripture and a message God encouraged me to share. Unlike other devotions, Beyond Words also includes a QR Code / Link for each day, taking you to a full-length piano worship cover that ties into the message and scripture.

I pray that these 30 days of devotion and piano worship would bring you God's overwhelming peace and joy, and that you wouldn't just be encouraged and reminded of

God's great love for you, but that you would feel called to pursue Him like never before.

HOW IT WORKS

Meditate on the Scripture

Each day begins with a passage of Scripture from the Bible. I suggest starting your devotion by meditating on God's Word. You can focus on the specific verse provided, or if you'd like to spend more time in Scripture, you can read the chapter in its entirety. (For example, if the verse of the day is Romans 8:28, read all of Romans 8.)

Read the Devotion

I share both big and small life and spiritual lessons that I've learned. I pray that they speak to you and encourage you in your walk with the Lord.

Reflection and Prayer

At the end of each day, you'll find a QR Code (physical book) or a Link (ebook). By scanning the code or clicking the link, you'll be brought to a private YouTube video of me playing a worship song that ties to the scripture and devotion for the day. As you listen, I encourage you to take some time to pray and reflect on the things God laid on your heart.

CONTENT

DAY
O N E

Romans 5:3-5

Not only so, but we also rejoice in our sufferings, because we know that suffering produces perseverance; perseverance, character; and character, hope. And hope does not disappoint us, because God has poured out his love into our hearts by the Holy Spirit, whom he has given us.

Let's admit it: Sometimes, life throws you curveballs. Some are small and sneak in without us noticing anything happened. Others are larger, and we swing for the fences and miss - big time. There are some curveballs, however, that are entirely unexpected and throw you into a tailspin. For me and my wife, 2019 felt like one monstrous, slow-moving curveball.

My wife Chantelle and I entered 2019 having just purchased our first home. (Hello, mortgage!) Soon after we signed the loan documents and grabbed the keys to our new home, I decided to stop playing for restaurants and private parties to focus on my growing YouTube channel. We started the year so excited about all of these new adventures in marriage and business. Then - almost out of nowhere - curveballs began to come flying at us from every direction.

In April, Chantelle went to the doctor for her yearly physical. She left the doctor's office, labeled a "star patient." Imagine our shock when she received a call a couple of days later to come back in to discuss unusual test results. Curveball number 1: a diagnosis of Type I Diabetes.

Curveball two came a couple of months later. The hand pain I had been dealing with for over a year exploded. What was once relatively manageable had become too much to bear. I visited various doctors and specialists and tried different methods and treatments to fix the issue, but nothing seemed to ease the pain.

The hard truth? I had overused my hands playing the piano. One of my most valuable tools was now at the point of breaking. The only treatment possibile? A half a year of complete rest.

Winter came, and Chantelle and I were convinced that we had exhausted our share of curveballs for the year.

Oh, how we were wrong. A few weeks into December, my Grandma Lee - who was my spiritual mentor - suffered a major stroke and was taken to the hospital in a medically-induced coma. I learned that she likely only had a few days left to live, and I knew I needed to go to Korea to be with her and my family during her last days on earth.

Unfortunately, traveling across the world costs money. I hadn't been working, and we were facing substantial medical bills that we hadn't built into our budget. I found myself looking at available plane tickets to Korea, and the results were devastating. It was going to cost over $3,000 to travel to reach my Grandma on such short notice.

Curveball, curveball, curveball. How can you keep on receiving curveballs even after you have struck out?

As I reflect on that year, I realize it would have been really easy just to give up and complain about all the challenges we were facing. But here's the truth that I learned amid those struggles: had I given up and thrown in the towel, I wouldn't have seen all the miracles and ways God was moving in our lives and marriage:

Chantelle's diagnosis taught us how to communicate better, rely on each other more, and learn to eat healthier.

When I couldn't play piano for six months, I discovered I was still a precious child of God - nothing I did or didn't do would change that reality!

When money was tight looking for plane tickets, we had friends come out of nowhere, helping foot the bill for my plane ticket to Korea.

Spending Christmas in Korea without Chantelle to attend my Grandma's funeral was one of the hardest things I've had to do, but it gave me the chance to celebrate Christmas with my family for the first time in over ten years!

I don't know what curveballs you've been dealt, or what surprise pitches may come your way in the future. However, I do know this: God is working in your life in and through the curveballs. Remember Paul's words in our reading today: we rejoice in our sufferings because they make us stronger, more faithful children of God!

Are your eyes and your heart open to see His overwhelming presence, His mighty miracles, and His never-ending love?

Scan the QR code to play
Day 1 Piano Worship Video

DAY
T W O

2 Corinthians 5:14-15, 20-21

For Christ's love compels us, because we are convinced that one died for all, and therefore all died. And he died for all, that those who live should no longer live for themselves but for him who died for them and was raised again...We are therefore Christ's ambassadors, as though God were making his appeal through us. We implore you on Christ's behalf: Be reconciled to God. God made him who had no sin to be sin for us, so that in him we might become the righteousness of God.

Want to know one of the reasons I absolutely love to play piano? Because no one is able to hear the lyrics while I play. I know that it can seem like a really funny reason to like piano, but I love how playing allows me to bring worship to people who would, otherwise, never have access to worship!

On more than one occasion, I have found myself playing a Piano Worship Video in a public setting and have had strangers come up and tell me that they love how passionately I play. What they don't realize is that I'm actually worshipping - and inviting them to share in that space with me. I think that's such a cool way to experience and enjoy the music!

This has made me think: shouldn't our lives as Christians be just as compelling to those that don't know God? I ask myself these hard, convicting questions often:

When I'm interacting with strangers, do they see the love and grace that Jesus shows me on a daily basis?

When strangers look at my marriage, do they see God's joy and peace?

When I meet someone for the first time, do they see God's humility and strength?

They say actions speak louder than words. If that sentiment is true, then I want everything I do to prove to others that God is real and that He is so, so good. There is nothing in this life that is not touched by God's great love for His precious children. Every "happy accident" has been perfectly orchestrated, and every blessing is a divine provision.

You are an ambassador of God, and as an ambassador, you are called to represent your King to the world! My prayer for you today is that every action you make will radiate God's goodness, love, peace, and joy to those around you. May you live so passionately that people can't help but notice and join in!

SHOULDN'T OUR LIVES
AS CHRISTIANS BE
JUST AS COMPELLING
TO THOSE THAT DON'T
KNOW GOD?

Scan the QR code to play
Day 2 Piano Worship Video

DAY
THREE

Joshua 6:2, 15-16, 20

Then the Lord said to Joshua, "See I have delivered Jericho into your hands, along with its king and its fighting men."...On the seventh day, they got up at daybreak and marched around the city seven times in the same manner, except on that day they circled the city seven times. The seventh time around, when the priests sounded the trumpet blast, Joshua commanded the people, "Shout! For the Lord has given you the city!"...When the trumpets sounded, the people shouted, and at the sound of the trumpet, when the people gave a loud shout, the wall collapsed; so every man charged straight in, and they took the city.

Sometimes, God will plant ideas and dreams in your heart that may seem, frankly, a bit crazy and impossible.

I experienced this kind of God-sized dream firsthand when I planned my music video for the song "Oceans." As I was arranging the piece, I couldn't help but think, "I should put a grand piano on the lake for this video!".

As exciting as it sounded, taking an incredibly heavy and valuable grand piano out in the middle of a lake didn't seem very realistic. We live in Northern Michigan, and at the time, it was the middle of cold, frigid January.

Still, I couldn't shake what God has placed in my heart. I felt in my soul that "Oceans" needed to be filmed on the water - even if it meant filming on ice.

Despite the freezing temperature and the situation's impossibility, I found a free grand piano that could be taken out onto a frozen lake! I set a date with my videographer and called all of my friends, asking for their help. Everything was set for what could be an incredible video!

The day before the video shoot, a massive snowstorm blew through, dumping 2 feet of snow on the lake. (Did I mention it was winter in Northern Michigan?) The forecast was calling for a high of -4 degrees Celsius! Yet the shoot went on.

When everyone showed up to the lake the next day, there was a lot of doubt whether this would actually work. Putting the piano out on the snow-covered ice seemed impossible. The ice fishers were even having a hard time getting through the snow, and they had a lot less weight to carry! There was no way this was ever going to work - right?

We know how the story ends when God places an idea in His people's hearts. It worked! With the help of about 20 friends, sleds, and snowmobiles - the grand piano found its way to the middle of the frozen lake. Once on the ice, we filmed one of the most unique and powerful music videos to date, touching millions of people worldwide.

There were multiple times I thought about calling the entire video shoot off. Even the morning of filming, seeing the weather outside, I wanted to give up or at least push off the video shoot. Yet Chantelle encouraged me to stick with the plan.

As we made our way to the lake, I kept thinking, "Is this going to be a huge failure? Will I end up wasting all of my friend's time and totally embarrass myself? What if the ice breaks and someone gets hurt?"

I started to pray and continued to pray throughout the morning. Thank God I didn't give up when every step felt more impossible than the last.

Sometimes, we're too quick to give up. We never see how things would have turned out if only we had trusted God's strength and vision.

Things might seem impossible through our human eyes, but when we look at it through the lens of God's perfect strength, we'll be able to keep pushing ahead without fear.

Scan the QR code to play
Day 3 Piano Worship Video

DAY
FOUR

Psalm 38:9

All my longings lie open before you, O Lord; my sighing is not hidden from you.

I don't know about you, but I love looking through the old pictures that I have stored on my phone and Instagram! Each time I scroll through them, they bring back so many forgotten memories. I just love seeing where I used to be and how things have changed.

I was scrolling through my photos recently and came across pictures from the summer of 2018. Looking at the pictures, I was reminded of how hard that summer was. Chantelle and I were saving for our first house and working like crazy to achieve our financial goals.

What made that season especially challenging,though,was our opposing schedules. Chantelle worked from 10am to 7pm and I worked from 5pm to 11pm. Even though we were working hard to achieve our dreams, we hardly saw each other.

As I was thinking about that difficult time, I kept scrolling through my pictures. As I scrolled, I started to realize that the further into summer I got, the more exhausted I looked in the photos. I guess I was more stressed out than I remembered.

Then I came across a new picture. The picture showed Chantelle and I both looking refreshed and happy, enjoying our time together on a special date.

A new memory came flooding back to me: We had both received the night off unexpectedly and had the opportunity to spend some much needed time together. Even then, God knew our deep need and blessed us with an extra-special dose of joy. As we finished dinner, we went to pay our bill, and were absolutely shocked when our waiter told us it had been covered by someone else!

From the unexpected night off to the spontaneous blessing of a stranger, we knew God was behind it all.

I'm so thankful we serve a God who cares about us so deeply. He's willing to send us personal reminders of His unchanging love for us. I'm so thankful we serve a God who is interested in every aspect of our lives. I stand in awe of the reality that God's love for us is just as apparent, if not more so, in the seemingly random blessings of life as it is in His miracles.

God cares. He loves you. His incredible moments of seeming coincidence are His unique way of showing you just how much you mean to Him!

Scan the QR code to play
Day 4 Piano Worship Video

DAY
FIVE

1 Peter 1:6-7

In this you greatly rejoice, though now for a little while you may have had to suffer grief in all kinds of trials. These have come so that your faith-of greater worth than gold, which perishes even though refined by fire-may be proved genuine and may result in praise, glory and honor when Jesus Christ is revealed.

Although I grew up in Seoul, South Korea, I now reside in a tiny city in Northern Michigan called Petoskey. In Petoskey, the summers are just about perfect. In fact, it's one of the reasons we rank so high on places you should vacation! However, this past year, we had a doozy of a storm terrifying tornado warnings and all!

As we watched the storm from the safety of our house, we saw giant trees (some probably hundreds of years old) being whipped back and forth by the wind. Massive branches were falling, and in some cases, the entire tree was lifted at the roots and pushed entirely over.

When the storm had finally passed, and the sun came out, Chantelle drew my attention to her flower garden. Incredibly, her lilies, rudbeckias, and all her wildflowers were standing completely upright - as if nothing had happened! How could these delicate little things weather the storm better than the strong and sturdy trees? I think the secret to their resilience is their willingness to bend and submit to the storm.

Isn't the same true for us? When we rely on our strength and power - when we insist that our way is not only the right way but the best way - we end up breaking apart during the severe storms of life. But if we submit our hearts to God and humble ourselves before Him, we can come through the storm standing tall!

No matter who you are, storms of different kinds are going to come your way. What is up to you is how you will react to the storm.

Will you try to stand strong in your strength and knowledge?

Or, will you submit everything to God, willing to bend to His ways, and see the storm as your refining fire? When you allow God to be the true Refiner of your life, He is faithful to shape and mold you into the strong and resilient child He has made you to be. Don't be surprised when you come out stronger and purer from the refiner's fire - God loves you too much to leave you unchanged!

THE SECRET TO THEIR RESILIENCE IS THEIR WILLINGNESS TO BEND AND SUBMIT TO THE STORM.

Scan the QR code to play
Day 5 Piano Worship Video

DAY
SIX

1 Chronicles 29:9

The people rejoiced at the willing response of their leaders, for they had given freely and wholeheartedly to the Lord. David the king also rejoiced greatly.

I learned a lot of excellent lessons from my parents growing up. Yet of all the wisdom and advice they gave me, one lesson in particular always brings a smile to my face when I think of it.

One Sunday, as I was getting ready for church in Korea, I came out of my room to show my mom my offering for the week. I was so excited because I had paper money to put in the offering plate this week! No more coins - I was finally moving up in the world!

I thought my mom would be so proud and excited for me, but she started to scold me when she saw my dollar bill. The paper money I was ready to give God was old, wrinkled, and worn. My mom quickly got out the iron and ironing board, handed them to me, and instructed me to flatten out my bill and make it look as best as I could for God. A few weeks later, I bought a mini-iron specifically for ironing all of my paper offerings.

As funny as it sounds, my wonderful mother taught me early that it's not about *how much* I give. It's about giving God my best and giving with a genuine heart, even in preparing the offering.

Today, I'm able to give a lot more than a single dollar each week. But to this day, I still find myself thinking about that particular Sunday morning lesson with the ironing board. As I reflect on the memory, I begin to reflect on my heart as well:

Did I prepare my heart for the offering I just gave?

Am I praising God with my finances, or only doing my "Christian duty"?

Am I just as excited about giving my money and heart to God today as I was 20 years ago?

I don't always give perfectly, but I get a little closer each time through this consistent act of self-reflection. As you prepare to give to God in the next few weeks - whether it's through time, money, or acts of service I encourage you to take a moment to reflect on how and why you're giving.

Remember today's scripture reading. Prepare your offering for God. Give with joy. Give your best. But most importantly, give your heart to God. That's what He wants from you more than anything else.

Scan the QR code to play
Day 6 Piano Worship Video

DAY
SEVEN

Revelation 3:15-16

I know your deeds, that you are neither cold nor hot. I wish you were either one or the other! So, because you are lukewarm - neither hot nor cold - I am about to spit you out of my mouth.

I know it may be cliche to say my dad is my hero, but it's true! I respect that man more than anyone else that I've known in my entire life.

My dad is a pastor in South Korea. As a pastor, he has dedicated all of his time, energy, and money to his congregation and the global church. His dedication to God, and the congregation God has given him, is like nothing I've seen before. It constantly inspires me to work harder and be better in pursuing my own unique calling from God.

These qualities definitely contribute to my respect for my father. But do you know what I respect even more? I love his rock-solid, crystal-clear convictions. No matter who has a conversation with my father, they can clearly see what he stands for and what he won't tolerate. Even more, whether he's talking to other pastors or strangers in a shopping center, he talks about his convictions full of love, kindness, and grace. People can't help but listen to what he has to say. Why? Because when gospel truth is spoken with love and gentleness, people start to recognize Jesus in their midst.

It's clear that our world is desperate and hungry for more of God, but there are a few traps we can be tempted to fall into. Sometimes we can be so concerned with not judging others that we compromise on our convictions. Other times, we are so firm in our convictions that we speak without love. Both of these are fatal to the Christian cause - not showing Jesus to those who need Him most.

It's time for us to stop being lukewarm, stuck somewhere in the middle in our conversations, our actions, and our convictions. Why would you ever want to be a hidden Christian? We have the greatest message to share in the world!

Don't leave others guessing what you stand for. Be so fire-hot that people can't help but notice you! When they do notice, speak with so much love, kindness, grace, and truth that all they can see is Jesus Himself! When they see the love and compassion of Jesus through your eyes, they won't be able to keep themselves from asking you why you live the way you do. How will you respond in that great moment of opportunity?

WHEN GOSPEL TRUTH IS SPOKEN WITH LOVE AND GENTLENESS, PEOPLE START TO RECOGNIZE JESUS IN THEIR MIDST.

Scan the QR code to play
Day 7 Piano Worship Video

DAY
E I G H T

Philippians 4:6-7

Do not be anxious about anything, but in everything, by prayer and petition, with thanksgiving, present your requests to God. And the peace of God, which transcends all understanding will guard your hearts and your minds in Christ Jesus.

Have you ever found yourself completely desperate for God's provision? So overwhelmingly stuck between a rock and a hard place, that you realize that the only way out is through a miracle from Heaven? I was in one of these places during my senior year of high school.

In high school, I knew that I wanted to study music when I graduated. However, I couldn't afford college application fees, so I saved up my money and only applied to one music school: Wheaton College. Wouldn't you know it, by God's grace I was accepted!

The impossible had been made possible through God! Well, except for the fact that they had to put me on the wait list because I couldn't afford the tuition. As an international student, the school required me to show my ability to pay all four years' costs at once!

I knew there was no way that I could possibly come up with that kind of money before school started - if ever! As an international student, I couldn't work a summer job and save like my peers, and my parents were already stretching themselves to afford one year of college, let alone four! I was stuck between a true rock and an impossibly hard place. My dream seemed stuck just out of my reach.

I spent most of my senior year in prayer. I prayed that God would lead me where He wanted me whether that was studying music at Wheaton, or back in South Korea, fulfilling my mandatory military service. I prayed for God's peace in the middle of so many unknowns. I prayed that my eyes would be opened to God's plans for me. I prayed for God to work miracles.

Wheaton College had given me an extension, but the day of the deadline eventually came. Despite our best efforts, we had still come up short. I was devastated. Suddenly, my phone started to ring, and I knew it was the call that would ask me if I had the money to attend school. I really wasn't looking forward to the hard conversation that lay ahead of me. I would have to tell them I couldn't attend that fall. We just didn't have the money.

I answered the phone with a heavy heart. However, the conversation that followed was nothing like I expected.

Incredibly, there was a donor who wanted to offer a scholarship specifically to an international student that couldn't afford tuition!

Amazing, right? But wait-it got even crazier! The amount of that particular donor's scholarship? It was the exact amount I still needed! WHAT?!

That was one of the most amazing moments of God's provision in my life. I can't even imagine how different my life would be right now, and I will forever be grateful for this miracle.

Are you in one of those spots right now? Do you feel like you'll never escape the dread and fear of tomorrow? Keep praying, and keep praying boldly!

Our scripture passage today tells us that we can trust God to act when we turn to Him with our anxious hearts and thoughts. Here is the truth that we must learn: God sees you, and He sees every need, He hears every prayer, and He knows each desire your heart holds.

Our God works miracles that we could never imagine, and He'll see you through this challenge - no matter how stuck you think you are! How will you share your anxious thoughts with Him today? Give it a shot, there is nothing hidden within that will scare Him away!

HERE IS THE TRUTH
THAT WE MUST LEARN:
GOD SEES YOU, HE SEES
EVERY NEED, HE HEARS
EVERY PRAYER AND HE
KNOWS EACH DESIRE
YOUR HEART HOLDS.

Scan the QR code to play
Day 8 Piano Worship Video

DAY
NINE

Ephesians 5:19b-20

Sing and make music in your heart to the Lord, always giving thanks to God the Father for everything, in the name of our Lord Jesus Christ.

You won't appreciate what you will have in the future if you can't appreciate what you have right now.

My father's ministry was just starting to grow as I was growing up in South Korea. My family didn't have a lot of money, and we were forced to move almost every year. Yet, as a child, I thought this way of life was totally normal and was completely happy with the way things were.

It wasn't until I started visiting friends at their homes that I started noticing my house was much smaller and that I had less stuff than they did. Why was this? Did my *lack* mean my life was *less*?

It's normal to want more and desire what you don't have. However, I praise God that my parents didn't focus on what they lacked during that stage of life. Instead, they fixed their eyes on the blessings God had given them at the moment. To this day, I'm convinced that this is why I have such a close and special relationship with my family, because my parents considered family as their greatest earthly blessing.

Now, 20 years later, the blessings that God is graciously pouring out on me and my family are even more apparent, overwhelming, and worthy of praise. Life is full of highs and lows, but even in the lows, we're surrounded by blessings from a God who sees every need, every want, and every desire.

Take a moment and think about all the things God has blessed you with today that money can't buy - your sense of sight and smell, family and friends, another day of glorious life. You are so richly blessed! Hold onto these blessings, these precious gifts, and choose to be thankful today so you can rejoice over the many blessings that are yet to come.

Scan the QR code to play
Day 9 Piano Worship Video

DAY
T E N

1 Corinthians 3:11-13

For no one can lay any foundation other than the one already laid, which is Jesus Christ. If any man builds on this foundation using gold, silver, costly stones, wood, hay or straw, his work will be shown for what it is, because the Day will bring it to light. It will be revealed with fire, and the fire will test the quality of each man's work.

So much in our lives changed when Chantelle was diagnosed with Type I Diabetes. However, the most significant change came in how we approach food each day.

As a person with diabetes, Chanelle has to be aware of her blood sugar levels at all times. If it drops too low, she can become weak and shaky and fall unconscious if she doesn't make a correction quickly. If it rises too high, she runs the risk of damaging her nerves and organs. What raises her blood sugar level? Sugar and carbs, which, when digested, turn into sugar.

Gone are the days we can give into every sweet-tooth craving, load up on large portions of pasta, and spontaneously grab a snack while out and about.

Now, we focus on eating a more plant-based diet and plan out our meals and snacks, making sure that each insulin injection matches the carbs that Chantelle is ingesting. We've become so focused on eating the correct amount of fruits and vegetables each day that we even bought a juicer! Not something you usually see in the kitchen of two twenty-something-year-olds!

Most interesting in all of this is the fact that everyone we know who has been diagnosed with an autoimmune disease or cancer has made the same drastic change to their diet. We are finally eating the way doctors have always told us to eat - but we only made those changes when it became too late for us to eat any other way.

Can the same thing be said of our relationship with Jesus? Are we running to Him every day because we want to be with Him, or do we wait until disaster strikes, and it's "too late" to do life alone?

If Jesus is truly the cornerstone of our life, then we should be building on Him every day of our lives - the good and the bad. All other cornerstones in life will fail us when the refining fires come. But with Jesus as our firm foundation, not only will we remain unshaken, but we will come out stronger and more like Him on the other side.

ARE WE RUNNING TO HIM
EVERY DAY BECAUSE WE
WANT TO BE WITH HIM,
OR DO WE WAIT UNTIL
DISASTER STRIKES?

Scan the QR code to play
Day 10 Piano Worship Video

DAY
ELEVEN

Galatians 5:25-26

Since we live by the Spirit, let us keep in step with the Spirit. Let us not become conceited, provoking and envying each other.

Can I be real with you for a moment today? Like, really, totally, completely transparent?

Often I feel like it's hard for me to make deep and real friendships.

My job is unique, and because it's unique, it comes with a whole set of challenges and opportunities that most people will never experience. There have been multiple times God has brought me fantastic opportunities. Still, I didn't feel comfortable sharing it with my friends because I didn't feel they genuinely wanted to celebrate my successes.

In some capacity, I get it. I've been that friend before. Too wrapped up in the comparisons, and too desperate to prove myself. There have been many times that I know I didn't see or celebrate what God was doing in and through my friends. This truth pains my heart. What's standing in our way of being open and honest with true friends?

I once heard a pastor say that we are so consumed with the need to not be ranked last that we would rather be first in an ugly world than last in a perfect world. That idea really hit home for me!

If we follow Jesus' example, and if we're following God's will for us, then this is the reality: God is always first, people are always next, and we are always last.

If we keep our eyes on Jesus, it doesn't matter if we are speaking to a classroom full of first-graders, a patient in a hospital bed, or before a packed auditorium at a Ted Talk - we all have reason to celebrate the amazing things that God is doing in and through us!

So, if you find yourself bound by comparison and longing to be first, I challenge you to take a step back. Stop looking at another's success through sinful human eyes, and ask God to soften your heart so you can truly celebrate the fact that God is doing something special for His purpose and Kingdom through you. How amazing is it to know that God is using you to accomplish His mission?

When you think about it, Jesus made sure He was last when He went obediently to the cross, making sure you came out on top! How much more should we live a Christ-like life, making sure that others come first no matter the circumstance? The more you become like Jesus, the more you will find that loving and serving others will bring you joy and fulfillment unlike any fame or fortune.

Scan the QR code to play
Day 11 Piano Worship Video

DAY
TWELVE

Ecclesiastes 2:11

Yet when I surveyed all that my hands had done and what I had toiled to achieve, everything was meaningless, a chasing after the wind; nothing was gained under the sun.

What are you chasing after in life?

A few years ago, I stumbled across a written account of Deion Sanders's life. His story really resonated with me. As one of the most gifted athletes in American history, Deion Sanders was one of the only athletes to compete in both the NFL and MLB championships.

Imagine that fame and success! Yet Sanders said that after winning a Superbowl and buying his dream Lamborghini, he felt completely empty inside. That vast emptiness he felt, coupled with a secretly failing marriage, led him to drive off a 40-foot cliff in an attempt to commit suicide.

Miraculously, Sanders survived. He emerged from the accident with only minor injuries and ultimately gave his life to God!

Just like Sanders, each of us is chasing after something. It may be studying hard to get into your dream college, working extra hours for a promotion, or saving for your very first home. There's always something we're running towards for purpose and happiness. However, at the end of our lives, all of these things will seem meaningless if God didn't call us to them.

True happiness and joy only come when we live our lives allowing God to direct our paths. If we follow the call God has for us, none of those things will be meaningless! We won't feel the emptiness Deion Sanders, felt because we'll be filled with the satisfaction and peace that only God can give!

So what are you chasing after right now?

Are you running towards what God is calling you to, or to what the world is calling you to?

The answer to those questions will make all the difference in your life today.

Scan the QR code to play
Day 12 Piano Worship Video

DAY
THIRTEEN

Genesis 3:14-15

So the Lord God said to the serpent,"Because you have done this, curse dare you above all the livestock and all the wild animals! You will crawl on your belly and you will eat dust all the days of your life. And I will put enmity between you and the woman, and between your offspring and hers; he will crush your head, and you will strike his heel."

Naengmyeon: a Korean cold noodle, vinegary soup; especially perfect on a hot summer day; quite possibly my very favorite food on the entire planet.

When it comes to Naengmyeon, I will literally go out of my way to eat this incredible dish whenever humanly possible.

We all have something in our lives that we prioritize more than anything else. Something that we intentionally make room and time for,and something we chase because it's just that important to us.

What's that one thing for you - that thing you drop everything to have or experience?

Now ask yourself - How would your life change if that one thing was God Himself?

Our God wants to be intentionally and relationally prioritized. He gives us so many perfect examples of how He's doing just that for us every day. Unfortunately, we don't always reciprocate the sentiment.

During COVID-19 and the lockdown that accompanied it, I often thought about how maybe this time was God's way of pointing out this fault to us. He cleared everything from our schedules, and while we sat at home, He waited to see if we turned to other idols or if we would run to Him.

Every circumstance is an opportunity for us to grow, not just personally, but in our relationship with God. Like a romantic relationship, if you don't intentionally prioritize the other person, you won't get to know them deeply. If you don't know their heart inside and out, you won't passionately love them with your whole self.

God wants to be your biggest priority. God wants to be your greatest love. How do I know this? Because in the very first pages of the Bible, after Adam and Eve prioritize themselves, God curses Satan before He gives them consequences for their sin.

How incredible is this? In that moment of deep betrayal, God was more concerned about restoring our relationship with Him than our punishment. Yes, He is holy and concerned with us living lives that reflect His goodness and purity, but He also makes it possible for us to live in communion with Him through the shed blood of Jesus on the cross.

Why did Jesus go to the cross? For you and me! You are His greatest priority! Is He yours?

Scan the QR code to play
Day 13 Piano Worship Video

DAY
FOURTEEN

Job 14:5

Man's days are determined; you have decreed the number of his months and have set limits he cannot exceed.

Everyone has some motto they strive to live by. Typically, I don't talk about my motto because people tend to immediately push back when they hear it. I'm sure it makes them uncomfortable, but that's the point!

So, if you find yourself wanting to dismiss what I'm about to say, I challenge you to pause instead and hear me out.

My motto is: *What if I die today?*

Take a moment to ponder this for yourself. Would you have any regrets if you unexpectedly died today?

That is definitely a tough question to ask, but I believe it's one of the reasons I'm so driven and relentless - I am inspired to live and experience each day to the fullest for God and His kingdom. Because at the core of this question is an even more important one:

If I die today, what would Jesus think about my life?

That's why this has become my motto. It helps me honestly evaluate every single part of my life my relationships, work, spiritual life, where I spend my time, money, and energy. To be completely transparent, the days I have regrets are also the days I'm living for my own glory.

That's precisely why I have to remind myself daily about what truly matters in the end. Because when I die, nothing else will matter other than Jesus' love for me. When I see Him face to face, I pray I can tell Him that I lived every day for Him - yearning to become His good and faithful servant. On that day, there will be no need for any explanations, because He will already know every thought, choice, and action I made.

So what if you die today? While we shouldn't live in fear, we should never take this life gift for granted. God makes it clear in His Word that our days are numbered.

Are you using your God-given gifts and resources to glorify His name?

Is God the center of everything in your life?

Are you living your life in its fullest to reflect God's perfection and holiness?

You are made in God's image, but are you an image-bearer of God?

God has written every single one of our days in His book of Life. With this truth in mind, we don't need to get upset about the little things. They're insignificant when looking at the big picture of all He is doing in our midst.

Live like today is your last day on earth, because it may be. Live with no regrets and no fear. Live a life that shows love and kindness to everyone you encounter. I pray that you can adopt this motto - *What if I die today?* - and pursue each day as a new chance to represent God and Jesus' love to a world in need of hope!

Scan the QR code to play
Day 14 Piano Worship Video

DAY
FIFTEEN

John 4:13-14

Jesus answered, "Everyone who drinks this water will be thirsty again, but whoever drinks the water I give them will never thirst. Indeed, the water I give them will become in them a spring of water welling up to eternal life."

I am a dreamer and an achiever.

These qualities have helped me create some truly unique business opportunities. However, in a society that puts so much emphasis and weight on results, it can also be a perilous thing for me.

There have been many nights that I have laid awake thinking about my results from that day, struggling with how I could have done better or done things differently and consumed with a feeling of desperation. I lay there, hoping that my results would live up to the standards of the world. This way of thinking quickly became unhealthy for me,and, if I'm honest, a bit debilitating.

As I struggled with these thoughts, I started to realize two things:

First, I had started believing the lie that my results were what made me valuable.

Second, I was more concerned with getting approval and affirmation from men when I really should have been focused on whether I was truly honoring God with everything that I did.

We all want to be accepted, heard, and respected, but the most significant affirmation we can receive is in knowing that God is pleased with us. God doesn't tell us, "Well done, my good and faithful servant!" only when we leave this earth. We have the opportunity to hear this affirmation from Him every single day.

If you seek affirmation from others, you will never be wholly released from your thirst. Instead, find satisfaction in turning your attention to God. When you take the time to listen to His voice, He'll tell you if He's pleased. If you are walking with Him, you'll hear more excellent affirmations than anything anyone else could tell you.

Today, will you stop drinking empty affirmations from a broken world? They may promise to bring you refreshment, but in the end will only leave you more dry and empty than before. Instead, turn to God - who gives graciously without limit - and never thirst again!

If you seek affirmation from others, you will never be wholly released from your thirst.

Scan the QR code to play
Day 15 Piano Worship Video

DAY
SIXTEEN

John 3:16

For God so loved the world that he gave his one and only Son, that whoever believes in him shall not perish but have eternal life.

Generosity - To be liberal in giving or sharing. Unselfish.

Chantelle and I have a fantastic and joyful marriage, especially considering the challenges of being a bi-racial couple. Coming from two different countries and cultures means that we face problems that are unique to our very different backgrounds. Our second year of marriage brought us one of these unique challenges in the form of generosity.

As many of you know, growing up in South Korea, my family didn't have much money. My dad was a pastor at a tiny church, and my parents have always been eager to give to the things God placed in their hearts. So the little money my dad made was given right back to the church and the missionaries they supported.

As I grew up, my parents felt led to send my older sister and me to the United States for high school and college. To help us make the expensive trip and establish our lives in the States, they used everything they had saved and took out loans to get us there.

I've always loved how open-handed my parents are with their possessions. So it broke my heart when I learned that the apartment building they were living in had been sold to developers. They needed to find a new place to live but didn't have the funds to do so. They needed our financial help.

My Korean heritage led me to feel that it was my duty to sacrifice for my parents. After all, they had sacrificed so much for my sisters and me!

However, as an American, Chantelle was not as convinced. It took many long, hard conversations to understand where the other person was coming from when it came to *generosity*. But I praise God for giving me a wife who's willing to listen and learn from my culture, set aside her financial goals for a short time, and learn how to be generous!

It was tough for both of us to help my parents with a new apartment's downpayment, but the most fantastic thing happened after we sent the money: our hearts followed our cash. Chantelle grew to love my family even more through the process because of her sacrifice for them.

Money is temporary, yet this financial sacrifice led to an eternal purchase: our generosity allowed Chantelle's love for my parents to grow.

Think of this challenging moment of generosity. How much greater is God's love for you? He didn't just send you earthly blessings. He sent you His only Son - a Son who would ultimately suffer and die a death you deserve so that you might have freedom instead!

Wow. Now THAT is the ultimate act of generosity. With that great truth in mind, if you ever find yourself in a position where it's hard to give, remember the unconditional love, sacrifice, and generosity that your Heavenly Father showed you when you needed it most.

Scan the QR code to play
Day 16 Piano Worship Video

DAY
SEVENTEEN

Isaiah 40:26

Lift your eyes and look to the heavens; who created all these? He who brings out the starry host one by one, and calls them each by name. Because of his great power and mighty strength, not one of them is missing.

When it comes down to it, we are just a handful of dust, mere humans.

In the middle of the country, our house is nestled at the bottom of a valley, making for some pretty incredible nighttime stargazing. Every time we go out to look at the stars, it's so clear. There is so little light pollution that we can see a strip of the Milky Way with our very own eyes! No matter how many times we look at it, it still manages to take our breath away.

But our God - this almighty, all-powerful creator of the universe - still chooses to call us "friend, son, and daughter."

Despite the vast list of wrongdoings under our name and all of our regrets, God willingly gave His life for ours and accepted us into His Kingdom - His family - teaching us what it really means to love.

Even more than the stars, God's love will never cease to amaze me. I'm just a handful of dust, yet, God pursues me every day, giving me what I desperately need but don't deserve. What can I not give back to Him for the unique gift of life He's given me?

This thought overwhelms my heart and leads me to pray the following prayer often. I wanted to share it with you today. Just like me, you're a handful of dust. And just like me, you have everything in God, and that is enough! I invite you to pray this prayer with me, and know that the God who created the stars and the heavens is listening to your prayer with such a great love that He sent His beloved Son to rescue you:

God, I will willingly give anything and everything you ask of me. There's nothing that gives me more joy than when I'm with you, living in your presence. Thank you for your mercy, your grace, and your never-failing love. You amaze me each day, and there's no place I'd rather be than simply with You. Amen.

Scan the QR code to play
Day 17 Piano Worship Video

DAY
EIGHTEEN

Jonah 1:12-17

"Pick me up and throw me into the sea," he replied, "and it will become calm. I know that it is my fault that this great storm has come upon you." Instead, the men did their best to row back to land. But they could not, for the sea grew even wilder than before. Then they cried to the Lord, "O Lord, please do not let us die for taking this man's life. Do not hold us accountable for killing an innocent man, for you O Lord, have done as you pleased." Then they took Jonah and threw him overboard, and the raging sea grew calm. At this the men greatly feared the Lord, and they offered a sacrifice to the Lord and made vows to Him. But the Lord provided a great fish to swallow Jonah, and Jonah was inside the fish three days and three nights.

Has God ever sent you His provision, but to your human eyes, it seemed like the furthest possible thing from what you were praying to receive? That's how I felt about the COVID-19 lockdown of 2020.

Chantelle and I had been praying about working together full time. We both shared the desire, but Chantelle was working 30-40 hours a week outside of the home, and we weren't sure how to transition from one to the other. Suddenly, seemingly overnight, the US was hit with a pandemic, and we were forced to stay home and self-quarantine. We found ourselves in a new position and lifestyle that we had never asked for!

However, something crazy happened. Being stuck at home, we were "forced" to work together full-time and make it work - no matter what! After a couple of weeks of trial and error, Chantelle found a clear role in my business. I must say, we were both blown away by the talent and versatility she possessed - something we would not have discovered if it weren't for the lockdown.

Just to ensure that I didn't miss this idea, God had me read through Jonah in my daily devotions. I've read through this story a million times, but it seemed like the words jumped off the page like never before when I read it this time:"But the Lord provided a great fish to swallow Jonah."

God provided the great fish! As we read later on in Jonah, God provided the vine and the worm that then ate that same vine! God continually provided exactly what Jonah needed every step of the way, and God has provided the same for me. That provision wasn't anything close to what I had in mind, but it was exactly what I needed.

God always answers our prayers, but we need to be willing to accept every answer - even when that answer looks drastically different from what we may have in mind. God's wisdom is unlike anything we can fathom, and His provision is always perfectly tailored to our situation, our needs, and to the hard lessons we need to learn.

Scan the QR code to play
Day 18 Piano Worship Video

DAY
NINETEEN

Psalm 10:4

In his pride the wicked does not seek him; in all his thoughts there is no room for God.

I used to take pride in how hard I worked. My life was built upon living out the entrepreneur hustle, the never-stopping, never-giving up pressure that our society preaches and worships. I was getting up early and staying up late, putting countless hours of work into chasing every vision that came into my head.

But then I started to realize something. This endless hustle had put my heart, mind, and focus on the wrong things. I talked about how I wanted to bring God the glory, but in reality, God wasn't the one being glorified - it was all focused on me and my work. My pride was getting in the way.

How often do we explain away our pride as something that's glorifying to God?

We say, "I'm only working this hard so God can be glorified.", but pride screams, "Look at how successful I am!".

We say, "My job is helping others, and therefore, glorifying God." but pride shouts, "Look at how generous and caring I am!".

We say, "I'm using my God-given gifts for God's glory." but pride is screaming, "Look at how talented I am!".

It took me a while to realize these prideful behaviors in my life. (Pride is sneaky like that.) However, when I dug deep and took a close look at my heart, I realized that my pride was putting the spotlight of focus and glory on me.

I started asking myself a series of questions every time I started to chase a dream or idea:

Why?
Why am I doing this right now?
Why do I want to accomplish this goal? Why is this dream important?"

We might convince ourselves that we don't have a pride issue, but God sees our heart's genuine desire and attitude. He sees our pride.

No matter what job you have, you have been skilled and equipped to worship and glorify the one true living God who gave us the gift of eternal life and salvation through His only Son, Jesus

Christ. Everything we do should be for His glory and His praise alone. Don't let pride stop you from worshipping the One who gave you everything!

Scan the QR code to play
Day 19 Piano Worship Video

DAY
TWENTY

Jeremiah 17:7-8

But blessed is the man who trusts in the Lord, whose confidence is in him. He will be like a tree planted by the water that sends out its roots by the stream. It does not fear when heat comes; its leaves are always green. It has no worries in a year of drought and never fails to bear fruit."

Chantelle and I recently celebrated our 4th wedding anniversary. The morning of the big day, I did the math and realised that we had actually been together for a total of 8 years!

(Yes, the math means that we started dating one month into our freshman year at college.)

The amount of time we've been together didn't surprise me. Instead, I was a bit taken aback by how much more clearly I understand what it means to depend on another person after so many years together.

From big to small, we've had plenty of opportunities to learn how to lean on the other in all things. For example, without Chantelle, I would be eating frozen chicken breast and rice for every meal. I 100% depend on her for yummy, well-cooked food.

Chantelle also has a keen sense of direction. There have been times I've driven right past our own driveway, not paying any attention to where I'm going. Chantelle is the reason I get anywhere successfully!

I'm also reminded of the time when we were on a jam-packed Chinese subway, rushing to catch a flight, and Chantelle suddenly fainted! She was (very subconsciously) trusting that I would keep her safe while not losing any of our luggage.

The day that Chantelle was diagnosed with Type 1 Diabetes out of the blue, she relied on me in a variety of ways: to remember what questions to ask new doctors, to help her count carbs and take the right amount of insulin, and to support her in this scary new journey.

But in America, where independence is one of the most excellent qualities a person can possess, learning to depend on someone else is one of the most challenging things to do. That is why I think marriage is one of the most beautiful examples God gave us - reminding us what our relationship with Him should look like.

Only when a husband and wife can completely trust and depend on the other will they experience the greatest joy and love this God-given life has to offer. Similarly, only when we learn to completely trust and rely on God in every aspect of our lives will we experience the greatest joy, love, and peace God has to offer.

Marriage, just like life, isn't always easy. It can actually be really, really hard. But the Bible is clear: we must depend on God in every area of our life. When we turn to him at every moment, he promises that we will be "planted firmly by streams of refreshing water." What a joy to know that God is always making a way for us to live in confidence.

What moment are you in right now? Are you bearing abundant fruit, or do you feel like you're in a time of draught? No matter what season we're in, we can't get ourselves anywhere without God's constant provision, grace, or mercy. Depend on Him. He's always there for you, ready to provide you with everything you need to thrive with joy.

Scan the QR code to play
Day 20 Piano Worship Video

DAY
TWENTY ONE

1 Thessalonians 5:16-18

Be joyful always; pray continually; give thanks in all circumstances, for this is God's will for you in Christ Jesus.

People often ask me how I live with such confidence and how I have been able to persevere in any situation. My secret? It's all about prayer.

Each morning when I wake up, I go through the same hour-long routine. Before I do anything else, I put on some quiet music, get on my knees, and pray for about 15 minutes. Then I read my personal statements, write in my journal, and read my Bible. Finally, I wrap up the hour with some physical therapy and plan out my day.

Now here is an essential element of my morning routine: It would be a lot more comfortable to pray on my knees after my physical therapy exercises, but I always begin with prayer. Why? Because I believe prayer is of utmost importance. It sets the tone for the rest of my day and aligns my heart with God's heart.

But prayer doesn't stop for me at the end of that hour. I pray in the afternoon when I'm faced with big decisions or simply to say thank you for something that happened. I pray in the evening when I feel tired and less motivated to get work done. Anytime something huge happens, if I feel anxious or unable to perform, or if I'm overcome with a thankful heart: I go to God in prayer.

I didn't just pick up this prayer habit overnight. Prayer is foundational to the Christian Church in South Korea, and my father (who was and still is a Pastor) taught me that I should respond with prayer in every circumstance. I'm so thankful he did!

Simply by praying, I find that I am more productive, and I know where to spend my time and energy. I have peace, I have confidence, and I can persevere in any situation. Why? Because through prayer, I'm communing with God - who is the source of my strength and power.

Will you rise to the challenge to pray like your life depends on it? As today's passage states, prayer isn't just something we do, it's God's will for us.

As you go about your day, your week, or even your month, I challenge you to create space specifically to pray. Bring all the big things, all the little things, every thought of gratitude to God. He will bestow on you a sense of peace, confidence, and understanding like never before!

Scan the QR code to play
Day 21 Piano Worship Video

DAY
TWENTY TWO

Romans 8:38-39

For I am convinced that neither death nor life, neither angels nor demons, neither the present nor the future, nor any powers, neither height nor depth, nor anything else in all creation, will be able to separate us from the love of God that is in Christ Jesus our Lord.

How is it that every single parent can look at their tiny baby and think they are the most amazing and precious thing on this earth, yet when you look at them yourself, you don't believe they are adorable at all?

It's because parents love their children for their inherent value.

This morning as I was praying, God reminded me of this truth: when we were born, we never had to earn love. We never had to worry about our looks, our work, or our talents. We were naturally, completely, and wholly loved by our beloved Father who created us.

Yet, somewhere along the way in life, we began to believe that the love we receive from others is based solely on our beauty, behavior, talent, and performance. It makes me sad to think of how many people live with this skewed view of worldly love every day and are suffering because of it. To be honest, this even includes me.

When I'm really honest with myself, I realize I do struggle with my image and how people view me through the lens of social media. It's easy to get caught up in what looks like glamor, but my identity should never be rooted in that!

Instead, my identity should always be rooted in the fact that I'm a Child of God! This is my inherent value that no one can take from me.

Today, I wanted to remind you that you are truly and deeply loved by your Heavenly Father, who created you and loved you long before you came into this world. You are fearfully and wonderfully made to be loved. The only thing that love is based on is your inherent value and identity in Christ.

People will always tell you what they think of you, but nothing you experience or do can separate you from the love of God as the Father. Why? Because you are a child of God. That is enough. Don't let anyone or anything ever take that away from you! With this confidence in mind, live today with more boldness and faith, knowing that you are wholly and completely loved.

WHEN WE WERE BORN,
WE WERE NATURALLY,
COMPLETELY, AND
WHOLLY LOVED BY OUR
BELOVED FATHER WHO
CREATED US.

Scan the QR code to play
Day 22 Piano Worship Video

DAY
TWENTY THREE

Colossians 2:6-7

So then, just as you received Christ Jesus as Lord, continue to live in him, rooted and built up in him, strengthened in the faith as you were taught, and overflowing with thankfulness.

My wife Chantelle has a beautiful flower garden planted in our backyard.She loves flowers and enjoys spending time outside, so the first summer as homeowners, I wasn't too surprised when the first thing she wanted to do was plant a garden.

Chantelle spent an entire day digging up a portion of our lawn, removing grass and weeds, installing a divider to keep weeds away, and laying mulch around the flowers she had planted. It was a ton of work, but knowing the most challenging part was over, I was excited to see what it looked like a few months later when the flowers were ready to bloom!

A few weeks later, I was confused when Chantelle was back in her little garden bent over her plants for an hour. Were the flowers already bloomed? Had she changed her mind? Was something wrong?

When I went to investigate, I found her weeding! Not much time had passed, but with birds and wind, weeds had found their way back in. Every weekend, Chantelle would make her way out to her garden to pull up weeds by the root.

Weeding a garden isn't a fun job, but it's a necessary one. If Chantelle doesn't invest the time to weed the flowerbed, her flowers will be choked out and die, and the weeds will flourish instead.

I think the same thing is true of our hearts. We've gone through the foundation work: learning about God, going to church, knowing what's right and wrong, even accepting Jesus as our Savior. But how many of us are actively weeding out the sin in our hearts?

Maybe we don't see it, or perhaps we've made excuses time and again. However, the fact remains: sin is planted in our hearts. If we're not careful, that sin will grow and flourish, choking out our faith that once flourished in our hearts for Jesus.

I'm happy to report that Chantelle's hard work in the yard has paid off. At the end of the summer, her garden exploded in colors and scents I couldn't have ever imagined!

The same can be true of our own lives and hearts. I encourage you to do the challenging but rewarding heart work. Ask God to open your eyes to the sin in your life that keeps popping up. It will be painful, and there will be times you want to give up, but you have no idea the kind of fruit you'll bear when the weed of sin no longer has a place to flourish.

Scan the QR code to play
Day 23 Piano Worship Video

DAY
TWENTY FOUR

Zechariah 2:13

Be still before the Lord, all mankind, because he has roused himself from his holy dwelling.

Life is BUSY! Can you relate?

I start each week with a clean page in my weekly planner, excited to enjoy some of the free time and potential adventures that each empty day promises. However, it doesn't take long for that page to fill up with commitments, meetings, deadlines, and my ever-expanding, seemingly endless to-do list.

Unfortunately, the "busy" doesn't stop when everything is crossed off the list. When I finally find a moment to stop and breathe, I find myself filling my life with more busy and more noise.

Think about it. How often do we have thirty minutes to slow down in our day, only to fill that space back up with

Facebook, Instagram, YouTube, News Updates, and TV episodes? Don't get me wrong; these fun activities can all be suitable for relaxing and winding down!

But are we using these distractions for our ultimate good? I'll be the first to admit that I'm usually using "fun" things to fill in the empty space most of the time.

It can feel awkward or uncomfortable for most of us to try and intentionally be still when life seems so busy and hectic. But ask yourself these questions:

Could the inability to relax be a sign that God isn't at the center of our hearts?

Has our relationship with Him become just another thing on our list waiting to be crossed off? Are we afraid to be still in His presence because we're scared of what we'll hear?

I'm not sure what the answer to these questions is for you, but if you find yourself running to anything other than God to fill in the empty space of your days, then I have a challenge for you.

Today, unplug, turn off, and put the phone or laptop away. Instead, stop and find a way to spend some time with God. Intentionally make Him your biggest priority.

God loves you so much and wants to spend time with you! This stopping and tuning in may feel awkward or uncomfortable at first, but those feelings will fade as your relationship with God grows and deepens. So press into that uncomfortable feeling! Your loving Father is waiting for you with open arms, and His to-do list only has one task: Spend time with His child.

Scan the QR code to play
Day 24 Piano Worship Video

DAY
TWENTY FIVE

Luke 6:45

The good man brings good things out of the good stored up in his heart, and the evil man brings evil things out of the evil stored up in his heart. For out of the overflow of his heart his mouth speaks.

In high school, some family friends bought a house that was in foreclosure. As they got closer to move-in day, they asked me if I would be willing to help them clean and move into their new home. I agreed!

I had driven past this specific house a few times and was always really impressed by it. The home is a large brick house, full of interesting details and large windows, and placed in a lovely neighborhood. However, when I showed up for the first day of cleaning and stepped through the front doors, I couldn't believe what I saw.

The inside of the house was DISGUSTING! The floor was littered with dust, and dead bugs covered everything! You couldn't see the floors, shelves, or counters underneath the layers of filth, and the decaying bug carcasses were staining everything a sickly yellow color. I realized now why it had been on foreclosure, and I was extremely thankful my friends were providing me with big yellow cleaning gloves!

How could something look so perfect on the outside, yet be so ugly on the inside?

Is the same true for us in our walk as Christians?

There have been times in my life where, from the outside, people have probably thought that I was a "good Christian". However, if they could see what was on the inside - if they could see my true heart - they would see disgusting yellow rot and decay.

Why would my friends buy this nasty house? The reason was apparent: they saw through the grime and the grit to the home's true potential. They put in the many hours of work needed to make it a livable, beautiful, and vibrant space. But before it could become what they envisioned, they had to commit to it and put in the hard, dirty work of cleaning it from the inside out.

Can you see the same potential inside of you? God sees it there. He's forgiven every sin and cleansed you in Jesus's perfect and holy blood! If you aren't aware of your potential, then you're the one holding yourself back.

Are you willing to commit all of yourself to God? Only when you turn your gaze to the Father and ask Him to guide your steps will you discover where your true source of joy and worth comes from.

Grow towards your heavenly potential, making your heart for God even more vibrant and alive - even more attractive than the outward appearance other people see! Then from your heart the love of God will pour out for all to see!

Scan the QR code to play
Day 25 Piano Worship Video

DAY
TWENTY SIX

Psalm 51:10-12

Create in me a pure heart, O God, and renew a steadfast spirit within me. Do not cast me from your presence or take your Holy Spirit from me. Restore to me the joy of your salvation and grant me a willing spirit, to sustain me.

When we first purchased our home, I was most excited to have the ability to play my piano without fear of disturbing my neighbors. While I have enjoyed that freedom immensely, never in a million years would I have thought that I would be most excited about the bunnies in my backyard.

Slowly, I have become consumed with a desire to befriend one of these little rabbits, trying to think of ways to get them to live within the walls of our fence and feed them carrots from my fridge.

But the squirrels around my house? Now that's a totally different story. These pesky squirrels keep finding new ways up onto our deck and roof, and I don't even want to think about all the damage they could do. After consulting with my father-in-law and brother-in-law about this pesky rodent problem, they convinced me that I needed to buy a pellet gun to help me fend off the squirrels. After a trip to FleetFarm and some target practice, I was officially ready to defend my home from these invaders.

However, I wasn't prepared for the emotions I felt after my first kill. Yes, I was getting rid of a "pest", but the small animal was also so cute. A few days later, I got another one. I still felt uncomfortable but knew I was doing the right thing.

As the squirrels kept coming, I kept going out with my pellet gun, and each time I took one out, I found myself feeling less and less remorse. It didn't take me very long to stop feeling guilty.

All of this got me thinking: How much other stuff have I become desensitized to as I've continued to repeat certain things over time?

Are there areas of sin in life - maybe even totally unknown and hidden - that are simply there because we've become desensitized to certain sin and evil in the world? Often I think it's easy for Christians to look at sin as black and white, a line that can't be crossed. Yet we often forget that our standards are subject to our human limitations and understanding.

One of the best ways to combat this is to prayerfully ask God to reveal sin in our life that we're not aware of deep inside of us. This prayer is a direct result of our desire to pursue righteousness and a pure heart - not because we want to stay within imaginary bounds - but as an offering to God. His grace, mercy, and love surpasses all of our understanding and limitations and will give us the strength to become victorious over all sin - known and unknown. Through His perfect guidance and grace, He will redeem every area of our life - even those we didn't realize needed redeeming!

Praise be to God for His willingness to restore to us the joy of salvation when we so often forget!

Scan the QR code to play
Day 26 Piano Worship Video

DAY
TWENTY SEVEN

Ephesians 4:31-32

Get rid of all bitterness, rage and anger, brawling and slander, along with every form of malice. Be kind and compassionate to one another, forgiving each other, just as in Christ God forgave you.

Have you ever felt like it was impossible to forgive someone? I have.

When I was looking for safety and stability at a time in my life, a dear friend hid some knowledge from me that put me in a potentially dangerous situation. I didn't know if it was a lapse of judgment on their end or an act of selfishness, but I knew one thing: I felt utterly betrayed.

I struggled a lot with completely forgiving them in my heart (mostly when I felt like they weren't as apologetic as they could be).

Didn't they see how they wronged me?

Didn't they see how they betrayed me?

Didn't they see how selfish they were being?

The list of questions and self-justification for my anger went on and on.

One day, God reminded me of a truth I had forgotten: Jesus not only forgave me when I betrayed Him, but He even died on the cross for me!

But did I see how I wronged Jesus? No.

Did I see how I betrayed Jesus? No.

Did I see how selfish I was in my relationship with God? No.

Yet, even when I didn't show remorse as I probably should have to God, Jesus held nothing back. God's great love and forgiveness poured out on me in the form of Jesus' perfect blood that was shed on the cross to cover all of my sins!

With this gospel-perspective, I was able to slowly, but surely, forgive my friend for their betrayal. We all do things in our lives that fracture our relationship with God. However, through Jesus' sacrifice on the cross, forgiveness and reconciliation is possible every single time.

Here's the hard truth: People will hurt us in life. Yet these momentary hurts can't compare to the multitude of ways we've hurt God. With His grace and mercy, we can forgive every wrongdoing because He first forgave us.

When you see how great your own forgiveness was, and how Jesus endured it all for you to know Him, then you will discover that forgiving others is not only easier, but a true joy. Who will you choose to forgive today?

Scan the QR code to play
Day 27 Piano Worship Video

DAY
TWENTY EIGHT

Matthew 25:20-21

The man who had received the five talents brought the other five. "Master," he said, "you entrusted me with five talents. See, I have gained five more." His master replied, "Well done, good and faithful servant! You have been faithful with a few things; I will put you in charge of many things. Come and share your master's happiness!"

I know I've said this before, but I really respect my dad. He's one of the greatest preachers I've ever known, and his constant drive for God's kingdom and his heart for his congregation blows me away every time I think about it.

For the last 20 years, he's been a small church pastor in the country just outside of Seoul. Since the beginning of its ministry, it's been on a plot of land that's located in a green belt. To help protect the land of this green belt, the Korean government has not allowed anyone to break ground and build. So, to have a church building, the church meets in a greenhouse *(literally a greenhouse)* every week.

Meeting in an open-air greenhouse means that it's frigid in the winter and blazingly hot in the summer! It's not comfortable at all, but this small congregation of about 30 people comes to church four times a week. Think of that - my dad has preached four different sermons every week for the last 20 years!

This preaching schedule seems totally crazy and inspiring to me, so I asked my dad how he's able to do this so consistently and so well. What my dad told me blew me away: *It's not about the number. It's about the quality of care you can give to what God has given you.*

To my father, it doesn't matter if it's the middle of winter, and only two people show up to church that night. He still prepares to preach to thousands of people because he treasures and values each person and soul that God brings him.

His passion and dedication have been so convicting to me. It made me realize that if I'm not focused on genuinely caring for and cultivating what God has given me, my heart isn't aligned with God's. But if my heart is connected to God, He will keep the fire burning, sustain me in all circumstances, and give me the strength to be consistently excellent for Him.

What has God called you to be obedient to today? What people and gifts has He explicitly given to you? In our reading, we see that the Master expects His servants to invest His talents with joy and intentionality. However, to God, it's never about the numbers - it's about your heart in the process of His calling for you.

He only made one *you,* because only *you* can accomplish the goal He created you to meet. Give it the most excellent care!

Scan the QR code to play
Day 28 Piano Worship Video

DAY
TWENTY NINE

2 Chronicles 7:14

If my people, who are called by my name, will humble themselves and pray and seek my face and turn from their wicked ways, then I will hear from heaven and will forgive their sin and will heal their land.

Growing up, my parents taught me how I should pray. I don't mean they taught me how to recite a prayer at each meal and before bed. They taught me the real power of prayer and how to pray vulnerable, honest, heart-exposing prayers.

Churches in South Korea have a robust prayer culture. There are prayer services each week where, for the better part of an hour, the entire congregation is praying their personal prayers out loud all at once. This prayer culture, along with my parent's dedication to teaching me to pray, has made prayer a massive part of who I am today.

I don't think prayer is ever meant to exclusively be away to get questions answered or away for us to get help when we really need something. Prayer certainly plays an essential role in both of these things, but I don't just pray when I want one of these two things accomplished.

For me, prayer is about opening up my eyes to truly see where God is in my life at that very moment. And since I'm always looking for Him, I'm always finding Him in each moment.

We have a terrible habit of being our own worst enemy in life. If we're not careful, we can become our own oppressors, holding ourselves hostage from inside our own heads. When we pray only to get answers or receive help, we start to believe a debilitating list of lies:

God doesn't really know my true desires.

God doesn't have my back in this.

I'm praying so much, and there aren't any answers!

God must not be close, or even here, right now.

These are alllies! God always knows, and God is always with us, even if we don't feel like He's there.
Could our real problem be that we can't see God because we're only looking for Him in one spot?

What would happen if you prayed prayers of thanksgiving and joy throughout the day?

Would your eyes be opened to the plethora of blessings from Heaven?

What would happen if you prayed every time you misplaced something, like your keys, phone, or glasses?
Would you see God leading you to where you need to be?
What would happen if you prayed prayers of frustration to God? "God, I can't believe_____just happened! God,_____is making me so annoyed right now!"

Would you see God when_____ is resolved?
These are all things we experience daily. Are we looking for God in these moments or just the overwhelming ones?

I believe that prayer is the best way to fix our eyes on God and what He's doing in our lives and the world around us. The more I pray, the more I see Him. The more I see Him, the more I become like Him and feel His love for me!

Will you take the time today to pray to God? Really pray to Him? When we come to the throne of our Maker, the Holy Spirit makes a way for us to experience and know God - and hear from Him in ways we never thought possible. Rest and hope in your prayers today!

Scan the QR code to play
Day 29 Piano Worship Video

DAY
THIRTY

1 John 5:14

This is the confidence we have in approaching God: that if we ask anything according to his will, he hears us.

My Grandma Lee and I were super close. She was my spiritual mentor, and I felt like I could talk to her about literally anything and everything! God has moved in some crazy ways in my own life, but compared to some of my Grandma's experiences, I seem tame!

My Grandma grew up during Japan's forced occupation of Korea and the Korean War. In the time of war and strife, education wasn't a priority for many people. Because of this reality, Grandma Lee never learned how to read and write - her only mission was to survive each day.

Years later, she was introduced to Christianity and began to attend church and worship services. Yet, she struggled to follow along. Friends would help her find the right passage in her Bible, but even then, she would silently move her lips while the rest of the congregation read aloud.

More than anything, Grandma Lee desired to read the precious words in her Bible. God washer everything, and she longed to be closer to Him more than anything else in life.

One night, she sat praying the same prayer again: begging that somehow she would be able to read her Bible unassisted. She desperately wanted to grow closer to God.

Grandma Lee was never sure if what happened next was a vision or reality, but the pages of her Bible started quickly flipping back and forth in front of her. When the pages finally stopped moving, she looked at the page in front of her and could read everything!

From that moment on, she could read her Bible! Her entire life, she couldn't read anything but her Bible. Show her a newspaper, menu, or advertisement - none of it made any sense to her.

But hand her a Bible? She could read every word!

Grandma Lee's heart desire was to be with God, and boy did God show up! When the root of our desires and requests are to be in community with God, I believe He will move mountains to reach you.

My Grandma Lee prayed and lived more boldly than anyone I know. Because of her passion and mission, she witnessed many miracles like this in her life.

Our scripture today reminds us that when we speak to God, He hears us, and longs to act on our behalf. You may not believe that praying can actually work, but when we hear the stories of those who have devoted their lives to turning their face toward God in faithful prayer, we can't help but be amazed at how He moves for His precious children.

Be like my Grandma Lee - be bold and fearless in your pursuit of Jesus. Do you trust Him?

Scan the QR code to play
Day 30 Piano Worship Video

ACKNOWLEDGMENT

Although there are many people I would like to acknowledge, I would like to take this space to thank my beautiful wife Chantelle.

From building the concept, to handling all of the detailed works involved in making this devotion come to life, Chantelle's dedication and earnest work made this project possible.

But even more importantly, her constant encouragement and pursuit of excellence pushed me to give my best to God and to our readers. Although there were times I had a little temptation to cut some corners and speed up the process, she reminded me whom I'm here to serve, and how they deserve nothing but our best.

I am often the face of our brand, however, Chantelle's humble and faithful behind-the-scenes work has been the true fuel to our driving force. I praise God for such a loving and talented wife who has a sincere desire to serve God's Kingdom. There is no greater joy and gift than having her as my partner for life and serving together.

About The Author

YoungMin You believes his life is a living testament to God's transformation power.

Growing up in South Korea, YoungMin never dreamed he would become a Top 10 Billboard Charting Artist or teach thousands of people all over the world how to play piano. In reality, YoungMin and his family didn't have much money while he was growing up, leading him to learn piano by watching YouTube videos.

Today, YoungMin is passionate about helping others come to know God's love, joy, and peace, and encourages them to live the abundant life God calls them to.

If you would like to learn more about YoungMin, his music, or his online piano course, visit him at:

🌐 www.youngminyou.com
▶ YoungMin You
f YoungMin You
🅾 @ youngminyou